50 Quick and Delicious Pasta Recipes

By: Kelly Johnson

Table of Contents

- Spaghetti Aglio e Olio
- Creamy Garlic Parmesan Pasta
- Pesto Pasta with Cherry Tomatoes
- Classic Spaghetti Bolognese
- Carbonara with Crispy Bacon
- Lemon Butter Shrimp Pasta
- One-Pot Garlic Butter Chicken Pasta
- Creamy Mushroom and Spinach Pasta
- Pasta Primavera
- Penne alla Vodka
- Spaghetti Puttanesca
- Caprese Pasta Salad
- Chicken Alfredo
- Spaghetti with Meatballs
- Pesto and Sundried Tomato Pasta
- Broccoli and Cheddar Macaroni
- Tomato Basil Pasta
- Sausage and Peppers Pasta
- Shrimp Scampi Pasta
- Ricotta and Spinach Stuffed Shells
- Zucchini Noodles with Pesto
- Cajun Chicken Pasta
- Beef Stroganoff Pasta
- Pasta Carbonara with Peas
- Spinach and Ricotta Tortellini
- Baked Ziti with Mozzarella
- Roasted Garlic and Tomato Pasta
- Shrimp and Asparagus Pasta
- Garlic Parmesan Penne
- Spinach and Feta Orzo
- Pappardelle with Ragu
- Roasted Red Pepper Pasta
- Chicken Marsala Pasta
- Sweet Potato Gnocchi with Sage
- Spaghetti with Clams (Spaghetti alle Vongole)

- Lemon and Ricotta Pasta
- Vegan Avocado Pasta
- Pasta with Roasted Butternut Squash
- Tuscan Chicken Pasta
- Sweet Italian Sausage Pasta
- Spaghetti with Anchovy Sauce
- Pesto Chicken Pasta
- Shrimp and Broccoli Alfredo
- Mushroom Stroganoff Pasta
- Spicy Arrabbiata Pasta
- Pasta with Sun-Dried Tomatoes and Basil
- Sweet Chili Shrimp Pasta
- Roasted Veggie and Chickpea Pasta
- Spinach and Mushroom Lasagna
- Capellini with Lemon and Basil

Spaghetti Aglio e Olio

Ingredients:

- 8 oz spaghetti
- 4 cloves garlic, thinly sliced
- 1/4 tsp red pepper flakes
- 1/4 cup olive oil
- Fresh parsley, chopped
- Salt and pepper to taste

Instructions:

1. Cook spaghetti according to package instructions.
2. Heat olive oil in a pan, add garlic, and sauté until golden.
3. Stir in red pepper flakes and cooked spaghetti. Toss well, garnish with parsley, and season with salt and pepper.

Creamy Garlic Parmesan Pasta

Ingredients:

- 8 oz fettuccine or pasta of choice
- 1 cup heavy cream
- 1/2 cup grated Parmesan cheese
- 3 cloves garlic, minced
- 2 tbsp butter
- Salt and pepper to taste

Instructions:

1. Cook pasta and set aside.
2. In a skillet, melt butter and sauté garlic. Add heavy cream and simmer.
3. Stir in Parmesan and cooked pasta, tossing to coat. Season with salt and pepper.

Pesto Pasta with Cherry Tomatoes

Ingredients:

- 8 oz pasta
- 1/2 cup basil pesto
- 1 cup cherry tomatoes, halved
- 1/4 cup Parmesan cheese, grated

Instructions:

1. Cook pasta and drain.
2. Toss pasta with pesto, cherry tomatoes, and Parmesan.
3. Serve with extra Parmesan and fresh basil for garnish.

Classic Spaghetti Bolognese

Ingredients:

- 8 oz spaghetti
- 1 lb ground beef
- 1 onion, chopped
- 2 cloves garlic, minced
- 1 can (14 oz) crushed tomatoes
- 1/4 cup red wine (optional)
- 1 tbsp Italian seasoning
- Salt and pepper to taste

Instructions:

1. Brown the ground beef in a skillet, then add onion and garlic.
2. Stir in crushed tomatoes, red wine, Italian seasoning, salt, and pepper.
3. Simmer the sauce and toss with cooked spaghetti.

Carbonara with Crispy Bacon

Ingredients:

- 8 oz spaghetti
- 4 oz bacon, chopped
- 2 eggs
- 1/2 cup grated Parmesan cheese
- Salt and pepper to taste

Instructions:

1. Cook pasta and set aside.
2. Fry bacon until crispy.
3. In a bowl, whisk eggs and Parmesan. Toss pasta with bacon and egg mixture, seasoning with salt and pepper.

Lemon Butter Shrimp Pasta

Ingredients:

- 8 oz linguine
- 1 lb shrimp, peeled and deveined
- 2 tbsp butter
- 1 lemon, zest and juice
- 1/4 cup Parmesan cheese
- Fresh parsley, chopped

Instructions:

1. Cook pasta and set aside.
2. Sauté shrimp in butter, adding lemon zest and juice.
3. Toss pasta with shrimp and top with Parmesan and parsley.

One-Pot Garlic Butter Chicken Pasta

Ingredients:

- 8 oz penne pasta
- 2 chicken breasts, diced
- 3 cloves garlic, minced
- 1/4 cup butter
- 1 cup chicken broth
- 1/2 cup heavy cream
- Salt and pepper to taste

Instructions:

1. Cook chicken in butter and garlic until browned.
2. Add pasta, broth, and cream, and cook until the pasta is tender.
3. Season with salt and pepper, then serve hot.

Creamy Mushroom and Spinach Pasta

Ingredients:

- 8 oz pasta
- 1 cup mushrooms, sliced
- 2 cups spinach
- 1 cup heavy cream
- 1/4 cup Parmesan cheese
- Salt and pepper to taste

Instructions:

1. Cook pasta and set aside.
2. Sauté mushrooms, then add spinach and cook until wilted.
3. Stir in heavy cream, Parmesan, and cooked pasta. Season with salt and pepper.

Pasta Primavera

Ingredients:

- 8 oz penne pasta
- 1 cup mixed vegetables (zucchini, bell peppers, carrots, peas)
- 2 tbsp olive oil
- 2 cloves garlic, minced
- 1/4 cup Parmesan cheese
- Fresh basil, chopped

Instructions:

1. Cook pasta and set aside.
2. Sauté garlic and vegetables in olive oil.
3. Toss pasta with vegetables, Parmesan, and basil.

Penne alla Vodka

Ingredients:

- 8 oz penne pasta
- 1 cup heavy cream
- 1/2 cup vodka
- 1/2 cup marinara sauce
- 2 cloves garlic, minced
- 1/4 cup Parmesan cheese
- Salt and pepper to taste

Instructions:

1. Cook pasta and set aside.
2. In a skillet, sauté garlic, then add vodka and marinara sauce.
3. Stir in heavy cream and simmer until thickened. Toss pasta in the sauce and sprinkle with Parmesan.

Spaghetti Puttanesca

Ingredients:

- 8 oz spaghetti
- 1 can (14 oz) crushed tomatoes
- 1/4 cup Kalamata olives, sliced
- 2 tbsp capers
- 4 cloves garlic, minced
- 1/4 tsp red pepper flakes
- Fresh parsley, chopped
- Olive oil

Instructions:

1. Cook pasta and set aside.
2. Sauté garlic in olive oil, then add tomatoes, olives, capers, and red pepper flakes.
3. Simmer the sauce and toss with cooked spaghetti. Garnish with parsley.

Caprese Pasta Salad

Ingredients:

- 8 oz rotini pasta
- 1 cup cherry tomatoes, halved
- 1/2 cup fresh mozzarella, cubed
- 1/4 cup fresh basil, chopped
- 2 tbsp balsamic vinegar
- 3 tbsp olive oil
- Salt and pepper to taste

Instructions:

1. Cook pasta and set aside to cool.
2. Combine pasta with tomatoes, mozzarella, and basil.
3. Drizzle with olive oil and balsamic vinegar, then season with salt and pepper.

Chicken Alfredo

Ingredients:

- 8 oz fettuccine pasta
- 2 chicken breasts, cooked and sliced
- 1 cup heavy cream
- 1/2 cup grated Parmesan cheese
- 3 tbsp butter
- 2 cloves garlic, minced
- Salt and pepper to taste

Instructions:

1. Cook pasta and set aside.
2. In a skillet, melt butter and sauté garlic. Add cream and bring to a simmer.
3. Stir in Parmesan and chicken, then toss with pasta. Season with salt and pepper.

Spaghetti with Meatballs

Ingredients:

- 8 oz spaghetti
- 1 lb ground beef
- 1/2 cup breadcrumbs
- 1 egg
- 1/4 cup Parmesan cheese
- 1 jar marinara sauce
- 1 tsp dried oregano
- Fresh basil for garnish

Instructions:

1. Mix beef, breadcrumbs, egg, Parmesan, and oregano. Form into meatballs.
2. Brown meatballs in a skillet, then add marinara sauce.
3. Simmer for 20 minutes. Serve over spaghetti, garnished with basil.

Pesto and Sundried Tomato Pasta

Ingredients:

- 8 oz pasta
- 1/4 cup basil pesto
- 1/4 cup sun-dried tomatoes, chopped
- 1/4 cup Parmesan cheese
- Olive oil

Instructions:

1. Cook pasta and set aside.
2. Toss pasta with pesto, sun-dried tomatoes, and Parmesan.
3. Drizzle with olive oil and serve.

Broccoli and Cheddar Macaroni

Ingredients:

- 8 oz elbow macaroni
- 1 cup broccoli florets, steamed
- 1 cup shredded cheddar cheese
- 1/2 cup milk
- 2 tbsp butter
- Salt and pepper to taste

Instructions:

1. Cook pasta and steam broccoli.
2. In a saucepan, melt butter, then add milk and cheese to create a creamy sauce.
3. Toss pasta and broccoli with the cheese sauce, season with salt and pepper.

Tomato Basil Pasta

Ingredients:

- 8 oz spaghetti
- 2 cups cherry tomatoes, halved
- 1/4 cup fresh basil, chopped
- 2 tbsp olive oil
- 1 clove garlic, minced
- Salt and pepper to taste

Instructions:

1. Cook pasta and set aside.
2. Sauté garlic in olive oil, then add tomatoes and basil.
3. Toss pasta with the sauce and season with salt and pepper.

Sausage and Peppers Pasta

Ingredients:

- 8 oz pasta
- 2 sausages, sliced
- 1 bell pepper, sliced
- 1 onion, sliced
- 2 cloves garlic, minced
- 1 cup marinara sauce
- Olive oil

Instructions:

1. Cook pasta and set aside.
2. Sauté sausage, peppers, onions, and garlic in olive oil.
3. Stir in marinara sauce, then toss with cooked pasta.

Shrimp Scampi Pasta

Ingredients:

- 8 oz linguine pasta
- 1 lb shrimp, peeled and deveined
- 4 cloves garlic, minced
- 1/4 cup white wine
- 2 tbsp butter
- 1/4 cup olive oil
- 1 tbsp lemon juice
- 1/4 cup parsley, chopped
- Salt and pepper to taste

Instructions:

1. Cook pasta according to package instructions and set aside.
2. In a skillet, sauté garlic in olive oil and butter until fragrant.
3. Add shrimp and cook until pink, then deglaze with white wine.
4. Stir in lemon juice and cooked pasta, toss to combine.
5. Garnish with parsley and season with salt and pepper.

Ricotta and Spinach Stuffed Shells

Ingredients:

- 12 jumbo pasta shells
- 1 cup ricotta cheese
- 1 cup spinach, cooked and chopped
- 1/2 cup grated Parmesan cheese
- 1 egg
- 2 cups marinara sauce
- 1 cup shredded mozzarella cheese
- Salt and pepper to taste

Instructions:

1. Cook pasta shells and set aside.
2. Mix ricotta, spinach, Parmesan, and egg. Season with salt and pepper.
3. Stuff shells with ricotta mixture and place in a baking dish.
4. Pour marinara sauce over shells, top with mozzarella, and bake at 375°F for 25 minutes.

Zucchini Noodles with Pesto

Ingredients:

- 4 zucchinis, spiralized into noodles
- 1/2 cup basil pesto
- 1 tbsp olive oil
- 1/4 cup Parmesan cheese
- Salt and pepper to taste

Instructions:

1. Sauté zucchini noodles in olive oil for 3-4 minutes until tender.
2. Toss with pesto and season with salt and pepper.
3. Serve topped with Parmesan.

Cajun Chicken Pasta

Ingredients:

- 8 oz penne pasta
- 2 chicken breasts, sliced
- 2 tbsp Cajun seasoning
- 1/2 cup heavy cream
- 1/4 cup Parmesan cheese
- 1/4 cup bell peppers, chopped
- 1 tbsp olive oil
- Salt and pepper to taste

Instructions:

1. Cook pasta and set aside.
2. Season chicken with Cajun seasoning and cook in olive oil until browned.
3. Add bell peppers, then stir in cream and Parmesan.
4. Toss with pasta, season with salt and pepper, and serve.

Beef Stroganoff Pasta

Ingredients:

- 8 oz egg noodles
- 1 lb beef sirloin, sliced
- 1 small onion, chopped
- 2 cloves garlic, minced
- 1 cup beef broth
- 1/2 cup sour cream
- 1 tbsp flour
- 1 tbsp butter
- Salt and pepper to taste

Instructions:

1. Cook egg noodles and set aside.
2. Brown beef in butter, then sauté onions and garlic.
3. Stir in flour, then add beef broth and simmer.
4. Mix in sour cream and season with salt and pepper.
5. Toss with noodles and serve.

Pasta Carbonara with Peas

Ingredients:

- 8 oz spaghetti
- 2 eggs
- 1/2 cup grated Parmesan cheese
- 1/2 cup peas, cooked
- 4 slices bacon, cooked and crumbled
- 2 cloves garlic, minced
- Salt and pepper to taste

Instructions:

1. Cook pasta and set aside.
2. In a bowl, whisk eggs with Parmesan cheese.
3. Sauté garlic in a little oil, then toss with pasta, peas, and bacon.
4. Remove from heat and stir in egg mixture until creamy.
5. Season with salt and pepper.

Spinach and Ricotta Tortellini

Ingredients:

- 8 oz spinach and ricotta tortellini
- 1 cup marinara sauce
- 1/2 cup grated Parmesan cheese
- 1/4 cup fresh basil, chopped
- Salt and pepper to taste

Instructions:

1. Cook tortellini and set aside.
2. Heat marinara sauce in a pan and toss in cooked tortellini.
3. Garnish with Parmesan and basil. Season with salt and pepper.

Baked Ziti with Mozzarella

Ingredients:

- 8 oz ziti pasta
- 1 jar marinara sauce
- 1 cup ricotta cheese
- 1 1/2 cups shredded mozzarella cheese
- 1/4 cup grated Parmesan cheese
- 1 egg
- Fresh basil for garnish

Instructions:

1. Cook pasta and set aside.
2. Mix ricotta, egg, and Parmesan.
3. Layer pasta, ricotta mixture, and marinara sauce in a baking dish.
4. Top with mozzarella and bake at 375°F for 25 minutes.

Roasted Garlic and Tomato Pasta

Ingredients:

- 8 oz spaghetti
- 1 pint cherry tomatoes, halved
- 1 head garlic, roasted
- 1/4 cup olive oil
- 1/4 cup fresh basil, chopped
- Salt and pepper to taste

Instructions:

1. Roast garlic in olive oil at 400°F for 25 minutes.
2. Cook pasta and set aside.
3. Toss pasta with roasted garlic, tomatoes, and olive oil.
4. Season with salt, pepper, and garnish with basil.

Shrimp and Asparagus Pasta

Ingredients:

- 8 oz pasta (linguine or fettuccine)
- 1 lb shrimp, peeled and deveined
- 1 bunch asparagus, trimmed and cut into 2-inch pieces
- 2 cloves garlic, minced
- 1 tbsp olive oil
- 1/2 cup white wine
- 1/4 cup heavy cream
- 1/4 cup Parmesan cheese
- Salt and pepper to taste

Instructions:

1. Cook pasta according to package instructions and set aside.
2. In a pan, sauté asparagus in olive oil until tender. Add garlic and cook until fragrant.
3. Add shrimp and cook until pink.
4. Pour in white wine and cook for 2-3 minutes.
5. Stir in heavy cream and Parmesan, then toss with pasta.
6. Season with salt and pepper to taste and serve.

Garlic Parmesan Penne

Ingredients:

- 8 oz penne pasta
- 4 cloves garlic, minced
- 1/4 cup butter
- 1/4 cup olive oil
- 1/2 cup grated Parmesan cheese
- 1/4 cup fresh parsley, chopped
- Salt and pepper to taste

Instructions:

1. Cook penne pasta and set aside.
2. In a pan, heat butter and olive oil, then sauté garlic until fragrant.
3. Toss cooked pasta in garlic butter mixture.
4. Stir in Parmesan and parsley.
5. Season with salt and pepper and serve.

Spinach and Feta Orzo

Ingredients:

- 8 oz orzo pasta
- 2 cups spinach, chopped
- 1/2 cup feta cheese, crumbled
- 1/4 cup olive oil
- 1 tbsp lemon juice
- 1/4 cup pine nuts, toasted
- Salt and pepper to taste

Instructions:

1. Cook orzo according to package instructions and set aside.
2. In a pan, sauté spinach in olive oil until wilted.
3. Toss orzo with spinach, feta, lemon juice, and pine nuts.
4. Season with salt and pepper to taste.

Pappardelle with Ragu

Ingredients:

- 8 oz pappardelle pasta
- 1 lb ground beef or pork
- 1 small onion, chopped
- 2 cloves garlic, minced
- 1/2 cup red wine
- 1 can (14 oz) crushed tomatoes
- 1/4 cup heavy cream
- 1/4 cup Parmesan cheese
- Salt and pepper to taste

Instructions:

1. Cook pappardelle pasta and set aside.
2. In a pan, cook ground meat, onion, and garlic until browned.
3. Add red wine and simmer until reduced.
4. Stir in crushed tomatoes, cream, and simmer for 20-25 minutes.
5. Toss pasta with sauce and top with Parmesan.
6. Season with salt and pepper to taste.

Roasted Red Pepper Pasta

Ingredients:

- 8 oz pasta (penne or spaghetti)
- 2 roasted red peppers, peeled and chopped
- 1/2 cup heavy cream
- 1/4 cup Parmesan cheese
- 2 cloves garlic, minced
- 1 tbsp olive oil
- Salt and pepper to taste

Instructions:

1. Cook pasta according to package instructions and set aside.
2. In a blender, puree roasted red peppers with heavy cream.
3. In a pan, sauté garlic in olive oil, then add the red pepper puree and simmer for 5 minutes.
4. Stir in Parmesan and toss with pasta.
5. Season with salt and pepper to taste.

Chicken Marsala Pasta

Ingredients:

- 8 oz fettuccine pasta
- 2 chicken breasts, sliced
- 1/2 cup Marsala wine
- 1/2 cup chicken broth
- 1/2 cup heavy cream
- 2 tbsp butter
- 1/4 cup fresh parsley, chopped
- Salt and pepper to taste

Instructions:

1. Cook pasta and set aside.
2. In a pan, cook chicken in butter until golden and cooked through.
3. Add Marsala wine, chicken broth, and heavy cream. Simmer for 10 minutes.
4. Toss pasta with sauce and chicken.
5. Garnish with parsley and season with salt and pepper.

Sweet Potato Gnocchi with Sage

Ingredients:

- 1 lb sweet potato gnocchi
- 1/4 cup butter
- 8-10 sage leaves
- 1/4 cup Parmesan cheese
- Salt and pepper to taste

Instructions:

1. Cook gnocchi according to package instructions and set aside.
2. In a pan, melt butter and sauté sage leaves until crispy.
3. Toss cooked gnocchi in sage butter and top with Parmesan.
4. Season with salt and pepper.

Spaghetti with Clams (Spaghetti alle Vongole)

Ingredients:

- 8 oz spaghetti
- 2 lbs fresh clams, scrubbed
- 4 cloves garlic, minced
- 1/2 cup white wine
- 1/4 cup olive oil
- 1/4 cup fresh parsley, chopped
- Salt and pepper to taste

Instructions:

1. Cook spaghetti according to package instructions and set aside.
2. In a pan, heat olive oil and sauté garlic until fragrant.
3. Add clams and white wine, cover and cook until clams open.
4. Toss spaghetti with clams and sauce, then garnish with parsley.
5. Season with salt and pepper to taste.

Lemon and Ricotta Pasta

Ingredients:

- 8 oz pasta (fettuccine or spaghetti)
- 1/2 cup ricotta cheese
- 1/2 cup lemon juice
- Zest of 1 lemon
- 1/4 cup Parmesan cheese
- 2 tbsp olive oil
- Fresh basil for garnish
- Salt and pepper to taste

Instructions:

1. Cook pasta and set aside.
2. In a bowl, mix ricotta, lemon juice, lemon zest, and olive oil.
3. Toss pasta with ricotta mixture and top with Parmesan.
4. Garnish with fresh basil and season with salt and pepper.

Vegan Avocado Pasta

Ingredients:

- 8 oz pasta (spaghetti or fettuccine)
- 2 ripe avocados, pitted and peeled
- 2 cloves garlic
- 1/4 cup fresh basil
- 2 tbsp olive oil
- 1 tbsp lemon juice
- Salt and pepper to taste
- Cherry tomatoes, halved (optional)

Instructions:

1. Cook pasta according to package instructions and set aside.
2. In a blender, blend avocados, garlic, basil, olive oil, and lemon juice until smooth.
3. Toss the cooked pasta with the avocado sauce.
4. Garnish with cherry tomatoes (optional) and season with salt and pepper.

Pasta with Roasted Butternut Squash

Ingredients:

- 8 oz pasta (penne or rigatoni)
- 2 cups butternut squash, peeled and cubed
- 2 tbsp olive oil
- 2 cloves garlic, minced
- 1/2 cup vegetable broth
- 1/4 cup heavy cream (or coconut cream for a vegan option)
- 1/4 cup Parmesan cheese (optional)
- Fresh thyme or sage for garnish
- Salt and pepper to taste

Instructions:

1. Preheat oven to 400°F (200°C). Toss butternut squash with olive oil, salt, and pepper, and roast for 25-30 minutes until tender.
2. Cook pasta and set aside.
3. In a pan, sauté garlic in olive oil, then add roasted butternut squash and vegetable broth.
4. Use a fork to mash the squash and stir in the cream. Simmer for 5-7 minutes.
5. Toss pasta with the sauce, then sprinkle with Parmesan and garnish with fresh thyme or sage.

Tuscan Chicken Pasta

Ingredients:

- 8 oz pasta (penne or spaghetti)
- 2 chicken breasts, sliced
- 1/2 cup sun-dried tomatoes, chopped
- 2 cups spinach, fresh or wilted
- 2 cloves garlic, minced
- 1/2 cup heavy cream
- 1/4 cup Parmesan cheese
- 1 tbsp olive oil
- Salt and pepper to taste

Instructions:

1. Cook pasta and set aside.
2. In a pan, cook chicken in olive oil until browned and cooked through.
3. Add garlic and sun-dried tomatoes, cooking for 2-3 minutes.
4. Stir in spinach and cook until wilted.
5. Add cream and Parmesan, then toss with pasta.
6. Season with salt and pepper and serve.

Sweet Italian Sausage Pasta

Ingredients:

- 8 oz pasta (rigatoni or penne)
- 1 lb sweet Italian sausage, casing removed
- 1/2 cup onion, chopped
- 2 cloves garlic, minced
- 1 can (14 oz) crushed tomatoes
- 1 tbsp tomato paste
- 1 tsp red pepper flakes (optional)
- 1/4 cup fresh basil, chopped
- Salt and pepper to taste

Instructions:

1. Cook pasta and set aside.
2. In a pan, brown sausage and cook until no longer pink.
3. Add onion and garlic, cooking until softened.
4. Stir in crushed tomatoes, tomato paste, and red pepper flakes (optional). Simmer for 10 minutes.
5. Toss pasta with the sauce, then garnish with fresh basil.
6. Season with salt and pepper and serve.

Spaghetti with Anchovy Sauce

Ingredients:

- 8 oz spaghetti
- 6-8 anchovy fillets, chopped
- 2 cloves garlic, minced
- 1/4 cup olive oil
- 1/4 tsp red pepper flakes
- 1/4 cup fresh parsley, chopped
- Salt and pepper to taste

Instructions:

1. Cook spaghetti and set aside.
2. In a pan, sauté garlic and anchovies in olive oil over medium heat until the anchovies dissolve.
3. Stir in red pepper flakes and cook for 1 minute.
4. Toss cooked pasta with the anchovy sauce and garnish with fresh parsley.
5. Season with salt and pepper and serve.

Pesto Chicken Pasta

Ingredients:

- 8 oz pasta (penne or fusilli)
- 2 chicken breasts, sliced
- 1/4 cup pesto sauce (store-bought or homemade)
- 1/4 cup sun-dried tomatoes, chopped
- 1/4 cup Parmesan cheese
- Salt and pepper to taste

Instructions:

1. Cook pasta and set aside.
2. In a pan, cook chicken until browned and cooked through.
3. Add sun-dried tomatoes and pesto sauce, stirring to combine.
4. Toss pasta with the pesto chicken mixture, then sprinkle with Parmesan.
5. Season with salt and pepper and serve.

Shrimp and Broccoli Alfredo

Ingredients:

- 8 oz fettuccine pasta
- 1 lb shrimp, peeled and deveined
- 2 cups broccoli florets
- 2 cloves garlic, minced
- 1/2 cup heavy cream
- 1/4 cup Parmesan cheese
- 2 tbsp butter
- Salt and pepper to taste

Instructions:

1. Cook pasta and set aside.
2. Blanch broccoli in boiling water for 2-3 minutes, then drain.
3. In a pan, cook shrimp until pink, then set aside.
4. In the same pan, melt butter, sauté garlic, and add heavy cream.
5. Stir in Parmesan and toss with pasta, broccoli, and shrimp.
6. Season with salt and pepper and serve.

Mushroom Stroganoff Pasta

Ingredients:

- 8 oz pasta (egg noodles or fettuccine)
- 2 cups mushrooms, sliced
- 1/2 onion, chopped
- 2 cloves garlic, minced
- 1 cup vegetable broth
- 1/2 cup sour cream
- 1/4 cup fresh parsley, chopped
- Salt and pepper to taste

Instructions:

1. Cook pasta and set aside.
2. In a pan, sauté mushrooms and onion until softened.
3. Add garlic and cook until fragrant.
4. Stir in vegetable broth and simmer for 5 minutes.
5. Add sour cream and mix until smooth.
6. Toss pasta with mushroom sauce and garnish with fresh parsley.
7. Season with salt and pepper to taste.

Spicy Arrabbiata Pasta

Ingredients:

- 8 oz pasta (spaghetti or penne)
- 1 can (14 oz) crushed tomatoes
- 3 cloves garlic, minced
- 1/2 tsp red pepper flakes (adjust to taste)
- 2 tbsp olive oil
- 1/4 cup fresh parsley, chopped
- Salt and pepper to taste
- Grated Parmesan cheese for garnish (optional)

Instructions:

1. Cook pasta according to package instructions and set aside.
2. In a pan, heat olive oil over medium heat and sauté garlic until fragrant.
3. Add red pepper flakes and crushed tomatoes. Simmer for 10-15 minutes to allow flavors to meld.
4. Toss the pasta with the Arrabbiata sauce.
5. Garnish with fresh parsley and grated Parmesan.
6. Season with salt and pepper and serve.

Pasta with Sun-Dried Tomatoes and Basil

Ingredients:

- 8 oz pasta (fusilli or farfalle)
- 1/2 cup sun-dried tomatoes, chopped
- 2 cloves garlic, minced
- 1/4 cup olive oil
- 1/4 cup fresh basil, chopped
- 1/4 cup Parmesan cheese (optional)
- Salt and pepper to taste

Instructions:

1. Cook pasta according to package instructions and set aside.
2. In a pan, sauté garlic in olive oil until fragrant.
3. Add sun-dried tomatoes and cook for 2-3 minutes.
4. Toss the cooked pasta with the sun-dried tomato mixture and fresh basil.
5. Garnish with Parmesan (optional) and season with salt and pepper.
6. Serve immediately.

Sweet Chili Shrimp Pasta

Ingredients:

- 8 oz pasta (linguine or spaghetti)
- 1 lb shrimp, peeled and deveined
- 2 tbsp sweet chili sauce
- 1 tbsp soy sauce
- 1 tbsp olive oil
- 1/4 cup fresh cilantro, chopped
- 2 cloves garlic, minced
- 1 lime, cut into wedges
- Salt and pepper to taste

Instructions:

1. Cook pasta and set aside.
2. In a pan, heat olive oil and sauté garlic for 1-2 minutes.
3. Add shrimp and cook until pink, about 3-4 minutes.
4. Stir in sweet chili sauce and soy sauce, tossing to coat the shrimp.
5. Toss pasta with shrimp and sauce, then garnish with fresh cilantro and a squeeze of lime juice.
6. Season with salt and pepper to taste and serve.

Roasted Veggie and Chickpea Pasta

Ingredients:

- 8 oz pasta (penne or rigatoni)
- 1 can (15 oz) chickpeas, drained and rinsed
- 1 zucchini, chopped
- 1 bell pepper, chopped
- 1/2 red onion, chopped
- 2 tbsp olive oil
- 1 tsp cumin
- 1/2 tsp paprika
- 1/4 cup fresh parsley, chopped
- Salt and pepper to taste

Instructions:

1. Preheat oven to 400°F (200°C). Toss zucchini, bell pepper, onion, and chickpeas with olive oil, cumin, paprika, salt, and pepper. Roast for 20-25 minutes.
2. Cook pasta and set aside.
3. Toss the cooked pasta with the roasted veggies and chickpeas.
4. Garnish with fresh parsley and serve.

Spinach and Mushroom Lasagna

Ingredients:

- 9 lasagna noodles, cooked and drained
- 2 cups spinach, wilted
- 2 cups mushrooms, sliced
- 1 jar (24 oz) marinara sauce
- 1/2 cup ricotta cheese
- 1/2 cup mozzarella cheese, shredded
- 1/4 cup Parmesan cheese, grated
- 1/4 tsp garlic powder
- Salt and pepper to taste

Instructions:

1. Preheat oven to 375°F (190°C).
2. Sauté mushrooms until softened, then add spinach and cook until wilted.
3. Spread a layer of marinara sauce in a baking dish, then layer with cooked lasagna noodles.
4. Add ricotta cheese, spinach and mushroom mixture, and mozzarella.
5. Repeat layers, finishing with marinara sauce and Parmesan cheese on top.
6. Cover with foil and bake for 25 minutes, then uncover and bake for another 10 minutes to brown the top.
7. Serve hot.

Capellini with Lemon and Basil

Ingredients:

- 8 oz capellini pasta
- 2 tbsp olive oil
- 2 cloves garlic, minced
- Zest of 1 lemon
- Juice of 1 lemon
- 1/4 cup fresh basil, chopped
- Salt and pepper to taste
- Grated Parmesan cheese for garnish (optional)

Instructions:

1. Cook capellini pasta and set aside.
2. In a pan, heat olive oil over medium heat and sauté garlic until fragrant.
3. Add lemon zest and juice, stirring to combine.
4. Toss the cooked pasta with the lemon and basil mixture.
5. Garnish with fresh basil and Parmesan (optional).
6. Season with salt and pepper to taste and serve.